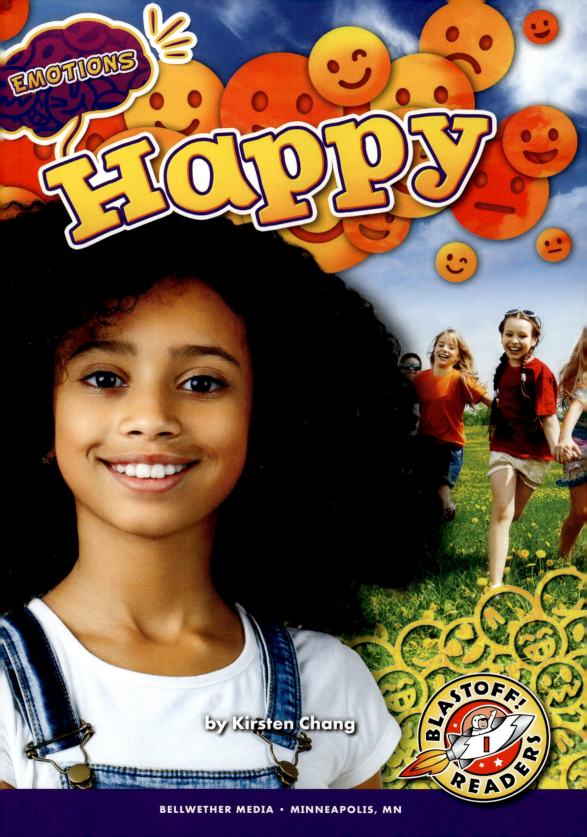

Blastoff! Readers are carefully developed by literacy experts to build reading stamina and move students toward fluency by combining standards-based content with developmentally appropriate text.

LEVELS

 Level 1 provides the most support through repetition of high-frequency words, light text, predictable sentence patterns, and strong visual support.

 Level 2 offers early readers a bit more challenge through varied sentences, increased text load, and text-supportive special features.

 Level 3 advances early-fluent readers toward fluency through increased text load, less reliance on photos, advancing concepts, longer sentences, and more complex special features.

★ **Blastoff! Universe**

Reading Level

Grade K

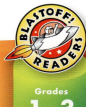
Grades 1–3

Grade 4

This edition first published in 2025 by Bellwether Media, Inc.

No part of this publication may be reproduced in whole or in part without written permission of the publisher. For information regarding permission, write to Bellwether Media, Inc., Attention: Permissions Department, 6012 Blue Circle Drive, Minnetonka, MN 55343.

Library of Congress Cataloging-in-Publication Data

LC record for Happy available at: https://lccn.loc.gov/2024014731

Text copyright © 2025 by Bellwether Media, Inc. BLASTOFF! READERS and associated logos are trademarks and/or registered trademarks of Bellwether Media, Inc. Bellwether Media is a division of Chrysalis Education Group.

Editor: Rebecca Sabelko   Designer: Andrea Schneider

Printed in the United States of America, North Mankato, MN.

Table of Contents

Time With Dad	4
What Is Happiness?	6
Being Happy	14
Glossary	22
To Learn More	23
Index	24

Time With Dad

Jack loves to draw with his dad. It makes him feel happy!

What Is Happiness?

Happiness is an emotion. You feel good when you are happy.

You may feel **positive** when you are happy. You may feel glad.

Isla feels happy when she plays with friends.

Kai is **grateful** when he spends time with family.

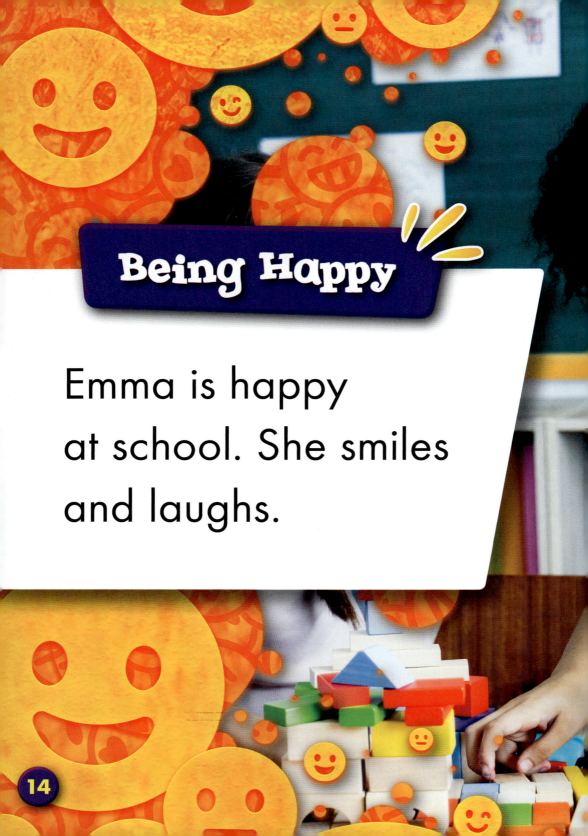

Being Happy

Emma is happy at school. She smiles and laughs.

Noah sings when he feels good.

Luna has a lot of **energy** when she is happy.

Be grateful when you are happy. It feels good to make someone else happy, too!

Glossary

energy
strength that helps you do things

positive
hopeful or thinking about things that are good

grateful
thankful

To Learn More

AT THE LIBRARY
Atwood, Megan. *Harper the Hare Feels Happy*. Minneapolis, Minn.: Jump!, 2024.

Chang, Kirsten. *Understanding Emotions*. Minneapolis, Minn.: Bellwether Media, 2022.

Lake, Theia. *Feeling Happy*. Buffalo, N.Y.: Enslow Publishing, 2023.

ON THE WEB

FACTSURFER

Factsurfer.com gives you a safe, fun way to find more information.

1. Go to www.factsurfer.com.

2. Enter "happy" into the search box and click 🔍.

3. Select your book cover to see a list of related content.

Index

draw, 4
emotion, 6
energy, 18
family, 12
feel, 4, 6, 8, 10, 16, 20
friends, 10
glad, 8
good, 6, 16, 20
grateful, 12, 20
identify happiness, 15
laughs, 14
plays, 10
positive, 8
question, 21
school, 14
sings, 16
smiles, 14
why are you happy, 11

The images in this book are reproduced through the courtesy of: Inside Creative House, front cover (happy child); Sergey Novikov, front cover (background), p. 11 (playing with friends); Daxiao Productions, p. 3; fizkes, pp. 4-5; ESB Professional, pp. 6-7; IndianFaces, pp. 8-9; Travelpixs, pp. 10-11; NDAB Creativity, p. 11 (spending time with family); Unai Huizi Photography, pp. 12-13; Streamlight Studios, pp. 14-15; Oksana Kuzmina, p. 15 (smiling); Olesia Bilkei, pp. 15 (laughing), 20-21; Robert Kneschke, pp. 16-17; FamVeld, pp. 18-19, 22 (energy); Peppersmint, p. 22 (grateful); Yuliya Evstratenko, p. 22 (positive); ViDI Studio, p. 22 (child with present).